Ernest
from

Trude.

Item
463.

301. MAR.

KU-429-501

ANTISEMITISM

JACQUES MARITAIN

ANTISEMITISM

GEOFFREY BLES: THE CENTENARY PRESS
37 ESSEX STREET, STRAND
LONDON

First Published in 1939

PRINTED IN GREAT BRITAIN BY THE WHITEFRIARS PRESS LTD
LONDON AND TONBRIDGE

FOREWORD

THIS essay is the development of a lecture given in Paris on February 5th, 1938, at the *Théâtre des Ambassadeurs*, under the auspices of the *Groupes Chrétienté*, and afterwards delivered by the author, with some additions which new events required, in New York, on December 14th, 1938, at the Cosmopolitan Club, under the auspices of the National Conference of Jews and Christians.

I am indebted to Mr. A. S. Oko, Dr. Emmanuel Chapman, Dr. Harry McNeill and Mr. Geoffrey Bles, for the revision they have made of the English text, and I here express my sincere gratitude to them, as well as to the publishers, who have been kind enough to publish this small book, revised and augmented according to a situation which is still in a state of flux.

PARIS, *April* 5, 1939.

ANTISEMITISM

In this short essay I propose to deal with the Jewish question and the situation of the Jews in the world of to-day. I shall treat this vast and distressing topic, conscious of my own inadequacy, but at least with all the insight which my reason and my faith can convey, and I shall treat it with that spirit of independence which we are determined to defend as our most valuable possession.

I shall speak first of special problems, arising from the situation of certain countries, out of which antisemitism is making capital; then of the dispersion of Israel in its divine significance, and at the same time, of the problem of antisemitism considered in its spiritual essence.

In a third section I shall deal briefly with factual questions of particularly grave urgency, that is to say, of the tragic situation in which the Jews at present find themselves in certain parts of Europe.

I

SPECIFIC ASPECTS OF THE PROBLEM

LET us consider, as briefly as possible, the concrete problems which make the Jewish question particularly acute, not so much in France, but in those countries which may be put into one of two categories: countries with a large Jewish minority, and countries, like Germany, where the great catastrophe following the war has been primarily diverted on to the heads of the Jews.

Countries with a large Jewish National Minority

In countries with a large Jewish national minority, it is obvious that the presence of an ethnic mass with its own traditions, schools and language, creates a special problem with regard to civil life and the general welfare of the State. This is true even in a country like Poland, which formerly welcomed the Jews with respect, and on several occasions invited them to furnish it with a middle class of artisans and traders, and in whose national culture the Jews have played a considerable part. And this problem is complicated, more or less seriously, when the old-established Jewish population is increased by waves of new immigrants. As a matter of fact, the statistics adduced by Polish and Roumanian antisemites regarding these more recent immigrations seem considerably exaggerated. Nevertheless, the problem exists, simply as a particular case of the general problem of national minorities, whose fate in contemporary Europe is often so cruel. In certain circumstances, especially where the Jews do not fit into the political scheme of the community, it can become extremely acute.

But I maintain that antisemitism *makes impossible* any solution of the concrete difficulties encountered in such cases. Not only does it falsify by exaggeration the factual data, but it removes the preliminary conditions required for any practical solution. For specific solutions can only be devised in an atmosphere of mutual understanding and collaboration, and the disease of antisemitism destroys the state of mind necessary in the very first place for such understanding on both sides; on the one side directly, and on the other by the passions of protest and resentment which it provokes in response, so that exasperation and misunderstanding, like reciprocal evils, grow irremediably in the minds of both parties.

Instead of offering purely political solutions to problems of a political order, antisemitism, even that so-called political antisemitism of which I am speaking at the moment, brings to bear on these problems already falsified beyond recognition solutions that are themselves false : laws of discrimination and measures of persecution inducing or designed to induce emigration *en masse*. And this is impossible.

In the first place, it is a confession of weakness for a State to resort to the extermination of certain elements of its population which it deems itself incapable of adapting to the service of the commonwealth. And further, it leads the way to greater difficulties in the future, because it signifies a corresponding diminution of internal energies, whose positive expression might have overcome those crises, which otherwise receive only an apparent cure from a surgical operation that is not even aseptic but, in fact, infected with hate and injustice.

For the justification of such false and illusory solutions, so-called *political* antisemitism employs a set of arguments which have no rational validity, but which have great emotional force, and which slip furtively over into *racial* antisemitism. Indeed, beginning with recent Jewish immigrants whom alone it first pretends to attack, it is extended little by little to Jews long established in the land, and to assimilated Jews, even to converted Jews, in short, to Jews as such, against whom it finally raises the racial myth. Let us say a few words about these arguments, which antisemitic propaganda is trying to popularise universally.

The Jews, it is said, crowd into a certain number of lucrative professions, notably the so-called liberal professions. So let them be driven out ! That will mean a certain percentage of competitors out of the way. However, there is the danger that they will be replaced by other competitors, surging up from the detestable swarm of humanity—even of non-Jewish humanity—who will thus threaten, dear antisemites, by their deplorable existence, not only your honest livelihood but also your innate sense of justice and of unselfish, spiritual and Western values. Into the bargain, it is plain that the Jews, unless one wants them all to die of hunger, must earn their living in some calling, and naturally they will be more numerous in those which suit them best. Everyone can forgive a natural irritation with successful competitors, provided it stays within reason ; but what arises here is clan hatred. Wherever there are Jews, they will be considered superfluous. What is really being denied them is purely and simply the right to exist.

Let us leave aside those voluntary agreements, which, in a really organic (pluralist) régime, could be reached with the Jewish community.* If you want to free certain professions of Jewish afflux, the best thing would be to endeavour to man them yourselves by showing more intelligence and diligence than the Jews, and by combating through some legitimate professional organisation, the abuses of free competition, whatever their source.

In this way competition between Jews and non-Jews would stimulate a raising of the cultural level, whereas recourse (equally humiliating for non-Jews and for Jews) to the brutal practice of the *numerus clausus*, let alone the *numerus nullus*, tends in itself to lower the level.

It is also said that Jews are given to usury, cornering the market, white slavery, and pornopraphic literature. Thus they are shown as the pernicious tempters of native populations, whose Christian fervour and virtues are displayed by our novelists, newspaper gossip columns and police-court reports. Through their press and publications, the Jews are responsible for the immorality sweeping over the nations of the world. The Jews go in for wicked political activities ; they are, of course, Communists—their presence *en masse* in the ranks of extreme Right terrorist organisations not having been exposed as yet.

" The Jews "—it is very natural for a man, especially some literary man or business man on whom one or two Jews have played a shabby trick, or who has noticed (among the large number of questionable personalities which life has thrown across his path) a few with Semitic profiles among many others who cannot be classified—it is very natural for such a man to say, not " *one Jew,*" or " *three Jews,*" or " *ten Jews* " with whom I have had

* See below, pp. 23–24.

5

dealings are this or that, but " *the Jews* " (of whom there are sixteen million in the world), " *the Jews* " are this or that. It is very natural, but it is hardly rational.

These summary turns of speech lead naturally to the worst sophisms. " *The Jews*," runs the antisemitic contention, *commit such and such crimes*. What sense is there in attributing to an entire community the individual faults of *some* of its members ? If, moreover, certain social evils, such as usury in some agricultural countries, are, as a result of national historical conditions, attributable especially to the Jews, other social evils which the antisemitic argument blames on " the Jews " reveal non-Jews as brilliant competitors. There is no need to mention further categories of social evils (such as alcoholism, crimes of violence, etc.), in which non-Jews clearly eclipse the Jews. Evil is done not by " *the Jews*," but by *some* Jews, and also by *some* non-Jews. What is the use of burdening one's conscience by infringing, in the case of the Jews, the elementary rules of law and of civilised life ? The social body must defend itself energetically against evils facing it, against a slanderous and corrupt press, against degrading publications. Quite so ! But the only effective way is to crush, if necessary by Draconian laws, all offences and abuses, no matter who has committed them ; not to strike a mass of innocents for the offences and abuses committed by some of their brethren and by others than their brethren, for abuses which would always find their votaries even if all Jews were exterminated.

Finally, as for the propagation of false ideas and false moral maxims, there would be reason to thank Heaven if " the Jews " (*some Jews*) were the only ones responsible ! We know very well that this is not the case, and that in the grand total the contribution of non-Jews is far greater than that of Jews. Herr Julius Streicher and other

6

instigators of pogroms are not Jews, and thus they with-
hold a powerful confirmation to their own argument,
which imputes to the Jewish race all the scourges of
humanity. Messrs. Rosenberg, Goebbels, and Hitler, and
the other armed disrupters of Western civilisation are not
Jews; Lenin was not one, nor is Stalin; and even that
vociferous French novelist, Monsieur Céline, who once
wrote *Voyage au bout de la Nuit*, is no Jew, although he
seems to have journeyed to the end of the night only to find
there the Protocols of Zion which awaited him, deposited in
those filthy shadows by the former Tsarist police.

I have mentioned the Protocols of Zion. Everybody is
aware that in Germany the Hitler propaganda machine
makes systematic use of this alleged document; everybody
also knows that this is the most impudent of forgeries, as
has been proved by all those who have seriously studied
the question, among others the prominent Jesuit, Father
Pierre Charles. If there are still orators and publicists who
dare to invoke this forgery to spread antisemitic legends,
one can only believe that they have lost respect for
their own intelligence and that of those who listen to
them.

To charge Jews with the sins of Bolshevism, to identify
Judaism and Communism, is a classic theme of Hitlerite
propaganda, which sometimes throws in Catholicism for
good measure. The theme is echoed with admirable
discipline by the antisemites of all lands. I do not believe
that in general the Jewish spirit, which these same mighty
brains reproach with harbouring an anarchic fever for
liberty, easily adapts itself to Communistic conformism.
What is true is that in some countries a section of Jewish
youth may find itself driven to revolutionary extremism
by the force of persecution. Those primarily responsible,

in such cases, are those who make their life unbearable. Thus, in a general way, those primarily responsible for supreme disorder are the false men of order, Jews and non-Jews, who, uniformly preferring injustice to disorder, base order on a fundamental, though at first concealed, disorder, thus offending the very principle of order and the Author of all nature.

We, as much or more than the antisemites (whose fury generally vents itself only on poor Jews), detest the hegemony of banks and finance, whether Jewish or non-Jewish, and no less the rule of money in any form. And here it is the materialistic structure and spirit of the modern world which horrifies us, whoever the individuals, Jews or non-Jews, who find themselves, generally without personal fault, involved in this inhuman structure. We know, moreover, that the great mass of Jews is made up neither of bankers nor of financiers, but of a population struggling against every form of urban poverty.

We do not underestimate the gravity of the great economic difficulties of our epoch and of the general economic crisis of civilisation. We say that it is not by hounding the Jews, but by transforming the economic and social structures, which are the real cause of those difficulties and of that crisis, that we can effectively remedy them. Antisemitism merely diverts men from the real tasks confronting them. It diverts them from the true causes of their woes—which lie simultaneously in our egoistic and hypocritical hearts and in the social structures causally inter-related to our moral poverty—antisemitism diverts men from the true causes of their sufferings to throw them against an innocent multitude, like a worthless crew which, instead of combating the tempest, would throw overboard some of their companions, until finally all are attempting to cut each other's throats and set fire to the vessel on which humanity lost in dreams has taken passage.

The German Drama

I have spoken of so-called political antisemitism and of the fertile soil which it finds in some countries with a large Jewish national minority. As a matter of fact, it is the example and contagion of German racism which for several years has distorted and aggravated, *bewitched* as it were, the conflict in such countries.

A pathetic and unfortunate nation, desperately longing to feel itself possessed of a common soul, the German people is also cast in a historic drama to which nobody with a sense of human solidarity can remain indifferent. Why must it, drawn by one of those magic melodies against which it has no power of resistance, to-day seek self-realisation by trampling on Jews and Christians—self-realisation, and doom ? This is not the place in which to expatiate on this drama. I will mention here only what relates to the Jews : if it be true (as the Jewish sociologist, Mr. Arthur Ruppin says, and as Karl Marx said with greater violence) that there is a sort of affinity and inter-relation between the Jewish spirit of adventure and the capitalist spirit of adventure, and if it be true that nowhere is Jewry more at home than in a capitalist civilisation *; and if, on the other hand, it be true that Germany, and above all post-war Germany, is the European country which has best known the wretched euphoria and the spiritual vertigo of a dislocated capitalism, one is less astonished by the paradox that, in Germany, an

---

* Whether we consider free competition, or interest paid on money loans, or price conceived as the result of discussion rather than as the expression of the objective value of a commodity ("just price "), we see ideas related to Jewish (and more generally to Oriental) economic conceptions, which the change from the medieval guild régime to the capitalist régime rendered predominant.

unprecedented tempest of hate has suddenly risen against the Jews, not because they remained aloof but, on the contrary, because they became assimilated, substantially assimilated to the German community to the extent of playing a major rôle in German culture and literature as such, and of sometimes forgetting their Jewish race and the woes of Israel. It is as though modern Germany sought, in her innermost being, to punish her own bad conscience in the person of the Jews, a stupefied scapegoat who cries out in vain : " But I live only for the power and glory of Germany ; I worship you alone, German greatness and German force in the service of a civilisation entirely dedicated to the conquest of power."

German civilisation, intensely and morbidly industrialised and deeply penetrated by the spirit of modern capitalism, after a crushing military defeat, reached general moral bankruptcy together with frightful material misery for its poor classes ; and in this people the poisons of humiliation have been nurtured and stored up. So this civilisation, neither finding nor even seeking an inner creative principle of a fundamentally new order, chose, instead of the Communist revolutionary catastrophe toward which its internal logic drove it, another revolutionary catastrophe which at least saved the State while losing everything else. It is not at all surprising that, entering thereafter upon a general régime in which illusion, myth and prestige replace and devour, as in an operation of black magic, the forms and functioning of real causes, it should instinctively give a special place to the anti-Jewish myth, which endows any fool with a means of explaining the misfortunes of history and of shifting on to somebody *guilty of everything*, the burden of his anguish and of his unhappy memories.

But if what I have just said is accurate, there is reason to believe that the relations between Germany and her Jews are more complex than appears. For neither the former nor the latter have changed—I mean really and basically. However persecuted, however humiliated, however abominably trodden under foot they may be, the majority of German Jews continues to cherish Germany, at least the Germany of the nineteenth century. As they weep by the waters of Babylon, it is not Zion that they recall, but pre-Führer Berlin, the Berlin of great capitalist adventure, of sublime intercourse with a prince of this world who had not yet donned the brown shirt of racial austerity. And, on the other hand, the Germany of Hitler, in seeking to reject Israel, has embraced the very worst of Israel. I mean that sentiment of racial pride which is, in some carnal Jews, the naturalistic corruption of the supernatural idea of divine election. Racists are indebted to the Old Testament as Communists are to the New. It is the Scriptures of the Jews from which the former drew, only to corrupt it, the idea of a chosen people, a people of God ; it is the Gospel from which the latter received, only to distort it, the idea of universal salvation and human brotherhood.

What I have just said must be well understood. I do not reproach the German Jews, as some have done so inopportunely, because they have not profited by Nazi persecution to be converted to Christianity. I simply say that they have not followed the example of their ancestors of the time of the prophets, have not sufficiently heard their cry in time of trouble to turn toward *their God*, and to remember *their origins*, which were in Abraham, Isaac and Jacob. Whether in Germany or out of it, they seem to have offered as a response to the terrible scourge which German racism has brought on the Jews, nothing but quite justifiable complaints and justifiable indignation, supplemented only by a call for an American boycott of German products and an appeal to international humanitarian literature. But that impulse of the heart which penetrates to the secret roots of history, that resurrection of spiritual forces in the face of which persecutors cannot stand and always end by admitting what they are, a bit of straw and blood-stained mud, can it be that Israel, surprised and perhaps paralysed by its rationalism, no longer knows or dares to put its trust in such a power?

Jews and Christians are curiously at one here. When they think of the state of affairs in Germany before 1933, are they not led to ask whether here, as in other lands, but with more immediately tragic consequences, there was not in too many of them a lack of a certain humble human compassion regarding those elementary realities whose terrible importance for our times has recently been indicated? Both in their respective ways privileged by divine adoption, did they not too tranquilly carry on *their business*, their business of earth and their business of heaven? Did they not fail to observe with sufficient sorrow the countenance of men and of the world decomposing before their very eyes, did they not fail to live close enough to the misery of men and of the world?

And now finally it is a new face, the sombrely ardent face of Paganism in man which is revealing itself. I do not wish to speak of these matters without paying tribute of admiration and brotherly love to the Christians of Germany, Catholics and Protestants alike, who suffer persecution like the Jews, and who are defying all dangers to defend against blasphemous rage both the Gospel and the Old Testament. Perhaps it is not commonly known, but it is a fact that a great many priests are now suffering, and suffering frightfully, in concentration camps. The bond of suffering in persecution has led both Christians and Jews to a consciousness of the fundamental bond uniting men, if not in their doctrine and rule of life, at least in that single origin which fashions them all in the image of God. The future will show what human history has been able to gain from such an experience.

But this essay is concerned particularly with the Jews. It is against them that racist neo-paganism first tried its strength. Its profound desire is undoubtedly, if that be possible, to drive every Jew out of the country. But since this cannot be done, it has to confine itself to depriving them of political existence and walling them up in a ghetto certainly more cruel than the ghetto of the Middle Ages, since men are now confined not because of a difference of faith and religion, against which free will and the grace of God always have recourse, but because of an irremediable difference of blood. Here we are faced with racial anti-semitism. To justify itself, it is not content to regard the Jews as a people, or as a race in the ethico-historical sense. They must be a race in the biological and anthropological sense of the word, and, at the same time, racism must become an ideology, a science, and a religion.

The truth is that the Jews are not a race in the biological sense of the word. We know that in man's present stage of development there is no group of any importance, even that most favoured in this respect, which is pure in race. The Jews are far from being an exception; mixtures of blood have, in the course of history, been as significant among them as among other human groups. Eminent scientists have concluded that, in man's present historic stage, the idea of race corresponds to no anatomical-physiological reality, to no unity of " blood," but merely to types of " mentalities " produced by historic and social

13

conditions. Its significance rests on extremely complex historical factors (of a psycho-ethico-sociological character) formed in the course of time, rather than on hereditary characteristics transmitted by blood.

Not that one need deny the existence of such characteristics, nor the importance of such a science as genetics and of such a psycho-physical basis as blood ; but these biological characteristics have been strongly intermixed in the ethnic brews compounded in the course of centuries, and in any case they are only a material element absolutely unqualified to constitute by itself a criterion of human value or to break the specific unity of the human family.

Scientifically, racism seems chiefly a sort of political distortion of anthropology, mobilised to furnish a practical criterion of the German national community.

Philosophically and religiously speaking, it is difficult not to see in this one of the worst materialistic mockeries of man. To claim, as was done at Nuremberg in 1933, that there is " a greater gap between the lowest forms which are still called human and our superior races, than between the lowest of men and the highest of monkeys," is not simply a philosophical absurdity. It is also an insult to the Christian faith which, in affirming the spirituality and the immortality of the human soul, in preaching brotherly love for men of all races and all conditions, in teaching that Christ died for the salvation of all, affirms at the same time the natural unity of the human species, its essential distinction from other species of animals, and the equal claim of all men to the title of children of God.

It is sometimes said, and I just used the word myself, that racism is neo-paganism : this is an insult to the pagans, who never lapsed into such brutish materialism. The cult of so-called predestined animal blood (in reality the vehicle of original sin and all those divisions among men of which this sin is the principle), is the cult most fundamentally opposed to the Christian cult of the redeeming and vivifying blood of the Word Incarnate, by means of which all who do not reject divine grace are brought into the supernatural unity of the " race " of God and the Sons of God.

From a social and cultural point of view, racism degrades and humiliates to an unimaginable degree reason, thought, science and art, which are thenceforth subordinated to flesh and blood and divested of their natural " catholicity." It brings to men, among all the modes of barbarism which threaten them to-day, a barbarism in itself the most inhuman and the most desperate of all. For, as I have just observed, it rivets them to biological categories and fatalities from which no exercise of their free will will enable them to escape.

II

THE DIVINE SIGNIFICANCE OF THE
DISPERSION OF ISRAEL

LET us now take up the question of the dispersion of
Israel, understood in its divine significance. As I wrote
in a recent study,* from which I am here borrowing several
pages, whatever may be the economic, political or cultural
forms, which are superficially covered by the problem of
the dispersion of Israel among the nations, this problem is
and remains in truth a sacred mystery, of which St. Paul,
in the Epistle to the Romans, gives us in a sublime summary
the principal elements.

If there are Jews among the readers of this essay, they
will understand, I am sure, that as a Christian I try to
understand, from a Christian viewpoint, something of the
history of their people. They know that, according to St.
Paul, we gentile Christians have been grafted on to the
predestined olive tree of Israel in place of the branches
which did not recognise the Messiah foretold by the
prophets. Thus we are converts to the God of Israel who
is the true God, to the Father whom Israel recognised, to
the Son whom it rejected. Christianity, then, is the over-
flowing expansion and the supernatural fulfilment of
Judaism.

The Vocation of Israel

Referring to the Jews, his brothers in the flesh to whom
he wished to be anathema, St. Paul had such a profound

* " L'Impossible Antisémitisme " appeared first in *Les Juifs* (Plon, 1937),
and later in our *Questions de Conscience* (Desclée De Brouwer, 1938).

and tender love for them " who are Israelites ; to whom belongeth the adoption as of children, and the glory, and the testament, and the giving of the law, and the service of God, and the promises ; whose are the fathers, and of whom Christ came according to the flesh," * that he wrote that " if the loss of them be the reconciliation of the world, what shall the receiving of them be, but life from the dead ? " † " For," continues the apostle, " I would not have you ignorant, brethren, of this mystery (lest you should be wise in your own conceits), that a blindness in part has happened in Israel, until the fullness of the Gentiles come in ; and so all Israel should be saved. . . . As concerning the Gospel, indeed they are enemies for your sake : but as touching the election they are most dear for the sake of the fathers. For the gifts and the calling of God are without repentance. For as you also in times past did not believe God, but now have obtained mercy through their unbelief, so these also now have not believed, for your mercy, that they also may now obtain mercy. For God hath concluded all in unbelief, that He may have mercy on all." ‡

Thus from the first Israel appears to us a mystery ; of the same order as the mystery of the world and the mystery of the Church. Like them it is a mystery lying at the very core of redemption. And we must say that, if St. Paul be right, what is called the *Jewish problem* is an *insoluble* problem, that is, one without *definitive* solution until the great redintegration foretold by the apostle, which will resemble a resurrection from the dead.

Between Israel and the world, as between the Church and the world, there is a suprahuman relation. It is only

* Rom. ix. 4.
† Rom. xi. 15.
‡ Rom. xi. 25, 26, 28–32

17

by considering this triad, that one can form some idea, even enigmatically, of the mystery of Israel. It seems to me that we have here as our sole guiding thread a sort of inverted analogy with the Church. We realise that the Church is not a mere administrative organisation dispensing religion. According to its own teaching about itself, it is a mysterious body in which living bonds, in order to accomplish a divine task, unite souls with one another, and with God. The Church is the mystical body of Christ. Indeed, Jewish thought is itself aware that in a quite different sense and in its own way, Israel is a *corpus mysticum*, a mystical body. A recent work by Erich Kahler, *Israel unter den Völkern*, emphasises this point particularly. The bond which unifies Israel is not simply the bond of flesh and blood, or that of an ethico-historical community ; it is a sacred and suprahistorical bond, of promise and yearning rather than of possession. In the eyes of a Christian who remembers that the promises of God are irrevocable and without repentance, Israel continues its sacred mission, but in the darkness of the world preferred on so unforgettable an occasion to the holy darkness of God. Israel, like the Church, is in the world and not of the world. But since the day when it stumbled, because its leaders chose the world, it is bound to the world, prisoner and victim of that world which it loves, but *of which* it is not, shall not be, and never can be. Thus is the mystery of Israel understood from a Christian viewpoint.

The communion of this mystical body is the communion of mundane hope. Israel passionately hopes, waits, yearns for the coming of God on earth, the kingdom of *God here below*. With an eternal will, a supernatural and non-rational will, it desires justice in time, in nature, and in the cities of man.

18

So, like the world and its history, Israel and its action in the world are ambivalent realities. Because the longing for the absolute in the world can take all forms, some good, others evil. Hence it comes that, in the astonishing complexity of the forms it assumes, simultaneously pregnant with good and evil, there will always be found something to glorify and something to degrade Israel. "Antisemites talk of the Jews," said Péguy. "Now I am going to venture on a paradox: antisemites know nothing about the Jews." Again, he said: "I know this people well. There is no portion of its epidermis that is not painful, where there is not some old bruise, some ancient contusion, some secret woe, the memory of a secret woe, a scar, a wound, a laceration of the Orient or of the Occident."

It is not a question of deciding whether you find Jews attractive or repulsive—that is a matter of temperament—but whether they have a right to common justice and the common brotherhood of man? If men could tolerate each other only on condition of having no complaint against each other, all the provinces of every country would constantly be at war. The most curious fact, moreover, is that many antisemites declare that they have only praise for Jews they have known personally, but nevertheless feel that it is a sacred obligation to hate the Jews. Which is one way, among others, of paying tribute to that mystery of Israel which we are considering.

But what, then, is that vocation of Israel which persists in darkness, and of which we were just speaking? First of all, there is its vocation as a witness to the Scriptures. But more, while the Church is assigned the labour of supernatural and supratemporal redemption of the world, Israel, we believe, is assigned, on the plane and within the limits of secular history, a task of *earthly activisation* of the mass of the world. Israel, which is not of the world, is to be found at the very heart of the world's structure, stimulating it, exasperating it, moving it. Like an alien body, like an activating leaven injected into the mass, it gives the world no peace, it bars slumber, it teaches the world to be discontented and restless as long as the world has not God ; it stimulates the movement of history.

The Spiritual Essence of Antisemitism

It seems to me that these considerations explain something of the spiritual essence of antisemitism.

The diverse particular causes which the observer may assign to antisemitism (from the feeling of hate for the foreigner natural to any social group, down to religious hatreds—alas, that these two words can be so coupled !— to the manifold inconveniences produced by some waves of immigration), mask an underlying spring of hatred deeper down. If the world hates the Jews, it is because the world clearly senses that they will always be " outsiders " in a supernatural sense, it is because the world detests their passion for the absolute and the unbearable stimulus which it inflicts. It is the vocation of Israel that the world execrates. To be hated by the world is their glory, as it is also the glory of Christians who live by faith. But Christians know that the Messiah has already conquered the world.

Thus hatred of Jews and hatred of Christians spring from a common source, from the same recalcitrance of the world, which desires to be wounded neither with the wounds of Adam nor with the wounds of the Saviour, neither by the goad of Israel for its movement in time, nor by the cross of Jesus for eternal life. We are good enough as we are, says the world, we have no need of grace or transfiguration, we ourselves will accomplish our own happiness in our own nature. This is neither Christian hope in a helping God, nor Jewish hope for a God on earth. It is the hope of animal life and its power, deep and, in a sense, sacred, demonic, when it masters the human being who thinks himself deceived by the emissaries of the absolute.

Racial tellurianism is antisemitic and anti-Christian. Communist atheism is not antisemitic : it is satisfied in being against God universally. In one as in the other, the same absolute naturalism, the same detestation of all asceticism and all transcendence, is to be found at work. It is the mystical life of the world which is to blossom heroically, as it were ; every mystical body constituted apart from the world must be rejected as such.

The French are not inclined to prostrate themselves before the world ; even when they lose their heads, it is in order to worship the goddess of Reason. That is why it seems to me that they will never be deeply antisemitic. They make fun of Jews as they do of their " curés," but genuine antisemitic mania never goes beyond the limits of a glorified petty bourgeois ideology. I do not overlook the violent propaganda being spread to-day in certain circles, I think artificially and sometimes venally. Those who know the French youth well, particularly the Catholic French youth, are confident that it will never march except in the name of liberty, generosity and intelligence.

Jews and Christians

Have I succeeded in giving some idea of the pathetic situation of the Jewish people ? Have I shown how, often despite itself, it manifests, sometimes in contrasting forms, a materialised messianism (which is the dark side of its dedication to the Absolute), but also admirable ardour, intelligence and dynamism, and so bears witness to the divine in human history ? Thence come the conflicts and the tension which, under all sorts of masks, necessarily prevail between Israel and the nations.

It is an illusion to believe that that tension can completely vanish ; but it is a villainy to desire to put an end to the problem by antisemitic violence (whether openly perse-cutory or politically mitigated)—one of those villainies natural to the human animal (whether he be an Arab and himself the descendant of Shem, or a Slav, a Latin or a German), and from which only Christianity, to the extent that it is really *lived*, can deliver the nations. The only way is to accept the state of tension and to face it in each specific case, not with hatred, but with that concrete intelligence which love demands from each, so that he may come to an early understanding with his adversary while they travel together, and in the consciousness that " all have sinned and need the glory of God," *omnes quidem peccaverunt, et egent gloria Dei.* " The history of the Jews," said Léon Bloy, " bars the history of the human race as a dyke bars the flood, in order to raise its level."

On the spiritual plane, the drama of love between Israel and its God, if we are to believe St. Paul, will reach a *dénouement* only with the reconciliation of the Synagogue and the Church. On the temporal plane, if there is to be no earlier truly definitive solution to the problem of Israel, there are nevertheless some partial or provisional solutions, particular responses whose discovery is the task of political wisdom and which each historic age must seek.

The period of history in which we live is for the Jewish people a time of accumulated difficulties. In the economic field the abandonment of free competition, the rise of *autarkia* and state capitalist régimes, deals a severe blow to Jewish industry and endeavour. Recently published studies of the economic situation of world Jewry indicate the growing pauperisation of the Jewish masses.

In the political and moral fields, the development of various types of totalitarianism, all of which regard the nonconformist as a biological enemy of the secular community, menaces the natural attachment of the Jews to independence and liberty.

In the spiritual field, the upsurge of unprecedented and ferocious forms of paganism signifies an inevitable conflict, already terribly begun, with that people who, though surrounded by the pagans of another epoch, knew how to pay heroic tribute to the sanctity of a personal and transcendent God.

I have come to believe that if the world should triumph over the errors and evils oppressing it to-day and should contrive to establish the rule of a civilisation, new and more consonant with human dignity, the solutions at once pluralist and personalist, which would have to prevail generally in such a régime, would likewise characterise those efforts which such an historic climate must inspire to regulate the Jewish question. As I tried to explain elsewhere,* a pluralism founded on the dignity of the human person, and established on the basis of complete equality of civic rights and effective respect for the liberties of the person in his individual and social life, would then recognise, in certain determined matters, an ethico-juridical status proper to various spiritual families, or even, sometimes, to various national communities which enter into the *convivium* of the temporal city. But such solutions (which though far removed from the old Liberalism, are

* Cf. " L'Impossible Antisémitisme," in *Questions de Conscience*, Paris, 1938, pp. 86–89.

thoroughly opposed to the ignominious mediævalist Hitlerian parody, and which tend to strengthen the links of justice and brotherly friendship between the various elements of the same civil society) could only be considered in a general new régime of civilisation, freed from the ills of capitalistic materialism as well as from the even greater ills of Fascism, Racism and Communism. Those who at present suggest a special status for the Jews are actually thinking of measures of discrimination against them. They are the victims of the absurd illusion, according to which the Jewish question (poisoned as are all the questions of to-day by the general crisis suffered by a civilisation which is sick and in a state of transformation) is the only or the principal cause of this crisis ; they imagine that the " solution " which consists of sacrificing the Jews would end the evils whose roots plunge, in fact, into the very depths of the economic, moral, spiritual and political structures of our civilisation. Infected by the contagion of the errors propagated by the racist mentality, they serve this mentality, whether they wish to or not. Some of them are fierce antisemites who pretend to be good apostles ; others protest that they are not antisemites, and consider themselves as dispassionate *realists*. One and all they are Herr Hitler's messengers, who have not even the excuse of passion.

Strictly speaking, the only suitable " realism " here would be that which understands the *reality* of the horror whereby the cult of hatred and the rejection of all human sentiment threaten the universe ; the only " realism " which a Christian has the right to profess in such a matter is the one that warns us that the least word which might convey the merest shadow of an indulgence or concession toward racism, runs the risk of assisting the Powers of Evil and of dripping with innocent blood.

24

If we now turn more particularly toward the Christians, it appears, that being themselves grafted on to the olive tree of Israel, they must look on the men involved in the Jewish tragedy with a brotherly eye and, as the apostle Paul teaches them, not without trembling for themselves. It is certainly possible for Christians to be antisemites, since one observes the phenomenon frequently enough. But it is possible for them only when they obey the spirit of the world rather than the spirit of Christianity.

Strangely enough certain Christians are heard to remark : " Has the world been moved, they say, by the massacres of so many Christians in Russia, Spain, and Mexico ? We will be stirred by the Jewish persecutions when the world will be stirred by the sufferings of our own."

When I hear this manner of reasoning, I wonder how it is that all of a sudden, and without anyone telling me anything about it, my religion has become changed. Does the Gospel teach us that if a brother has sinned against me, by omission or otherwise, it is justifiable to sin against him in the same fashion ? Jesus said : " These things you ought to have done, and not to leave those undone." Now it is said : " Because these things have been left undone, you ought not to do those." Because certain people have been lacking in justice and in love, others must be similarly deficient. . . .

Besides, it is not true to say that the world remained indifferent to the suffering of Christians in Russia, Spain and Mexico.* It is, however, true to say that many who to-day are full of indignation because of Racism remained quite cold regarding the discriminatory laws enacted by certain governments against religious Orders, and regarding

* Notably, various rabbinical organisations in the United States and France protested against the persecutions of Christians, as was revealed in a news release of the *Catholic Worker*, December 5th, 1938.

the anti-Christian persecutions which have raged or are raging in so many countries. I object to such unjust indifference and such one-eyed pity; but I do not want to lay myself open to the same objection.

Among careless or partisan writers many historic confusions arise from the intermingling in medieval civilisation of the affairs of the Church and the affairs of a secular Commonwealth religiously organised, where mundane interests and both the good and evil of human social life were steeped in religion. If one makes the proper distinctions, one can see that, in a temporal civilisation where the régime of the ghetto—not to speak of the drama of the Marranos and the Spanish Inquisition—lent itself to the worst antisemitic passions and excesses, the Church itself and as such (apart from a few of its ministers) was not responsible for these excesses.* It is well enough known that the Popes repeatedly defended the Jews, notably against the absurd charge of ritual murder, and that all in all the Jews were generally less unhappy and less badly treated in the Papal States than elsewhere.

Western civilisation, emerging from the Holy Roman Empire and the medieval régime, while in danger of collapsing in other respects, as we know, freed itself from the gross impurities which this régime brought in its wake; and it would be a singular aberration if Christians wished to return to those impurities at the moment when they have lost their historic reason for existing. To-day antisemitism is no longer one of those accidental blemishes of a temporal Christendom in which the evil was mixed

* If we avoid a unilateral selection of texts, and if there were sufficient acquaintance with the philosophy of history, it would be understood that neither the policy adopted at certain periods regarding the Jews by medieval Christendom, nor the supervening mistakes and abuses which may have occurred, prove that the Catholic Church is bound to antisemitism. I mention this for the benefit of certain Italian Fascist writers, as well as for certain American anti-Fascist writers. . . .

with the good; it is an error of the spirit contaminating Christians. I recall to the reader's mind that in a document of the Holy Office dated September 5th, 1928, which was directed against the mistakes of a too zealous " Association of the Friends of Israel," the Catholic Church explicitly condemned this error of antisemitism. Racist errors were again condemned (April 13th, 1938) in a pontifical document (letter of the Sacred Congregation of Seminaries and Universities).

It is well known that Pope Pius XI spoke out vigorously against the racist campaign and racist measures inaugurated by the Italian Government in imitation of the German Government. To the concept and word *race*, figuring in the theories imported from Germany, he opposed magnificently the ancient Latin ideas of *gens* and *populus*, the connotation of which belong much more to the moral than to the biological order.

The following passages of a discourse pronounced in September, 1938, before the directors of the Belgian Catholic Radio Agency are also to be noted. Commenting upon the words of the Canon of the Mass *sacrificium Patriarchæ nostri Abraham*, the sacrifice of our father Abraham, the Pope said, " Notice that Abraham is called our Patriarch, our ancestor. Antisemitism is incompatible with the thought and sublime reality expressed in this text. It is a movement in which we Christians can have no part whatsoever. . . . Antisemitism is unacceptable. Spiritually we are Semites."

Spiritually we are Semites. No stronger word has been spoken by a Christian against antisemitism, and this Christian is the successor of the apostle Peter.

As for its moral characterisation from the Catholic viewpoint, antisemitism, if it spreads among those calling themselves disciples of Jesus Christ, seems to be a pathological phenomenon, which indicates a deterioration of Christian conscience when it becomes incapable of accepting its own historic responsibilities and of remaining existentially faithful to the high exigencies of Christian truth. Then, instead of recognising the trials and shocks of history as the visitations of God, and instead of shouldering those burdens of justice and charity demanded by that great fact, it turns aside to substitute phantoms relating to an entire race, phantoms which derive a certain consistency from various real or fancied pretexts ; and in giving free rein to feelings of hate which it believes justified by religion, it seeks for itself a sort of alibi.

It is no little matter, however, for a Christian to hate or to despise or to wish to treat degradingly the race from which sprung his God and the Immaculate Mother of his God. That is why the bitter zeal of antisemitism always turns in the end into a bitter zeal against Christianity itself.

" Suppose," wrote Léon Bloy, " that people about you were to speak continually of your father and your mother with the greatest contempt, and to have for them only insults or outrageous sarcasms, what would be your sentiments ? Well, that is exactly what is happening to Our Lord Jesus Christ. We forget, or rather we do not wish to know, that as a man Our Lord was a Jew, the epitome *par excellence* of the Jewish nature, the Lion of Judah ; that His Mother was a Jewess, the flower of the Jewish race ; that the apostles were Jews, along with all the prophets ; finally, that our whole liturgy is based on Jewish books. How, then, can we express the enormity of the outrage and the blasphemy involved in vilifying the Jewish race ? "

III

THE PRESENT TRAGEDY OF THE JEWISH PEOPLE

Everybody knows that the Jews miss no opportunity for lamentation. If they are such adepts at weeping, it is because they have a sempiternal habit of sorrowing and because they are disarmed. To-day, in any case, it may be said that, in the matter of persecutions, they are plentifully supplied.

The third part of this essay, in which I shall speak of matters of fact concerning the actual situation of the Jews in various countries, will obviously be but a brief summary. If one were to enumerate in detail all the types of oppression involved, one could never conclude.

Before examining briefly the effects of antisemitism in Germany, Rumania and Poland, let us say a few words about the situation of the Jews in Russia.

The Jews in Russia

Perhaps some people will say in surprise : But does not the U.S.S.R. make a boast, and justifiably, of having officially proscribed antisemitism ? Has it not given the Jews, as it has members of other ethnic groups, equality in law and free access to schools and universities ? Yes, that is true. Nevertheless, Russia is one of the countries of the world in which Israel is most threatened.

I do not here speak simply of the economic ruin which

c 2

the Soviet régime brought on the Jewish masses. Ninety per cent. of the Jews of Russia lived from trade, industry and crafts. Their means of livelihood have been harder hit than those of the peasant masses, because the new régime no longer tolerates merchants or independent craftsmen. For them the economic disaster is complete.

No, what I want to point out above all is that, if *the Jews* can live, however miserably, in Russia, *Jewry* and *Judaism* are condemned to death. Their assimilation, forced assimilation, is succeeding only *too well*.

Here the struggle has not been, and is not being, carried on against the Jewish race, but against the Jewish religion, as against all religions. Violent persecution, conducted by some atheist Jews, has burst on religious Jews. "Here," one Jewish author writes, "it is the Jew who is the Jew's worst enemy." Finally, the great mass of Jewish youth is cut off from religion. Only the older generation perseveres, but, "in the face of the hostility of the governing classes, it dare not move, and religion is doomed."

"In this country," writes the same author, "where the Jews twenty years ago were still the most solid bulwark of Judaism, the Jewish religion is about to be destroyed." *

And, by the same token, Jewish culture is doomed. Rabbinical schools and almost all synagogues are closed. Teaching in the Hebrew tongue, folklore, religious holidays, circumcision, the rites of the Mosaic law, all are practically forbidden. A mighty State pressure works, on the other hand, in favour of mixed marriages, with the result that the Jewish ethnic and cultural entity is rapidly vanishing.†

Likewise, Zionism, regarded as an "imperialist" move-

---

* Arthur Ruppin, *The Jews in the Modern World*, New York, 1934.

† In the Jewish State—that is to say, in the region populated by Jews—which the Soviets have tried to create in Birobidjan, specifically Jewish culture is languishing.

ment, is rigorously repressed, and every attempt at Zionist propaganda becomes the object of immediate arrest and exile.*

It was recently said of Yiddish literature that its force and originality "come from *its impotence not to be religious.*"† In a general sense, there is no Jewish culture and no Jewish people without the God of the Scriptures, if His presence be only in the dead bones of a tradition devoid of faith, which Zionism, at least, respects and preserves.

It is a remarkably significant phenomenon and one which confirms our earlier reflections, that everything proceeds as though a profound hatred of the Scriptures, wherein God testifies to Himself, rebounds on Israel itself as a mystical body, and Israel, as a mystical body, is never afflicted without Israel, as a people, feeling the same blow.

The Jews in Germany

We have dealt with German racism in its principles. Is it necessary to recall now how it works out in practice?

According to the law of April 7th, 1933 (that of the famous *Aryan clause*), supplemented by other legislative acts of the same year, all non-Aryans, that is to say, all human beings who bear in their veins 100 per cent. or 50 per cent. or—when they have had a single Jewish grandfather or grandmother—25 per cent. of Jewish blood, are barred from public posts as well as, either directly or indirectly and by means of persecution, from the liberal and "cultural" professions.

Jews have been forbidden to participate in the world of the theatre, the Press, literature, music destined for the Aryan masses, or to become teachers or students in German

* Olav Leroi, *La Croix*, January 30th to 31st, 1938.
† Paul Fierens, *Revue des poètes catholiques*, No. 1, 1937.

universities. They are the objects of special laws, not to unite them to the life of the commonwealth, but to segregate them as an inferior and noxious race.* Let them work out for themselves a ghetto culture ; but even if they were to be encouraged to do so, it would be as slaves are encouraged to sing songs to themselves before death comes. Let them devote themselves to commerce ; but even if some of them were to hold important positions, in many sectors of economic life they are dispossessed for the benefit of Aryans. Jewish shops are boycotted ; Aryans guilty of buying from Jewish merchants are threatened and molested ; Jewish birth alone becomes a valid reason for the discharge of any employee.

Blood dominates everything, dominates intelligence and goodwill, grace, and baptism. The children of a baptised Jew must be taught in a Jewish, not in a Christian school.

We know that in September, 1935, the Nuremberg laws, those "laws for the protection of German blood and honour," deprived the Jews of the title of citizen and of political rights. We know that the same laws forbid marriage (as well as extra-marital sexual relations) between Jews and non-Jews under penalty of prison and hard labour. These punishments having proved insufficiently efficacious, some antisemites propose now to institute capital punishment for the crime of what they call *race shame* or *racial pollution*.

Let us cite here, as an example, certain facts which were collected by Louis Roubaud, a French journalist endowed

---

* It is notable that the Jews form but a small proportion of the German population. Before Hitler came to power there were in Germany about 550,000 Jews. From 1933 to the end of 1937, according to the careful statistical studies of Dr. Kurt Zielenziger of Amsterdam, published in the review *Population*, about 135,000 Jews left Germany. Some 30,000 went to other European countries, the rest to Palestine, South America, the United States and South Africa.

with great objectivity, during an inquiry recently made by him in Germany, and which he published in the *Petit Parisien* (March, 1939) :

"Posters warn imprudent citizens : 'Every girl so forgetful of her race as to visit a Jew or to receive him in her house, or to go for a walk with him, will be shaved and exposed in the public square. We invite Germans conscious of their dignity to watch over Christian women who cultivate a Jew, to give us their addresses, and to inform us of their behaviour.'

"Such punitive exhibitions are a current spectacle for citizens of large and small towns.

"I passed but one day in Nuremberg, and I was coming out of my hotel when such a procession passed before me. . . . I first beheld six soldiers in arms, pushing in front of them a young boy in women's clothes ; but it was not a boy, but a girl, completely bald, and yet pretty, with blue eyes bright with tears, and so thin and fragile ! After having shaved her head, the soldiers had hung round her neck a sign : 'I HAVE GIVEN MYSELF TO A JEW.' She was exhausted, stumbling. Having arrived before the hotel, she let herself fall on the greasy pavement, pretending to have fainted. They kicked her to make her get up, and one of the kicks marked her delicate face with blood and mud. . . . I had the courage to join the loiterers who were following. When she was really unable to walk any more, the soldiers lifted her on their shoulders to show her to the distant spectators. . . .

"The Fritsche trial is not an exceptional case. Herr Fritsche, a widower of forty-five, is the father of a boy of eighteen, a 'boy in uniform,' like many others, and who is undergoing training in camp with others. Herr Fritsche, a decent fellow and fond of sport, is not an old man.

Sarah was his wife's friend. She is thirty-five and pretty. The honest affection which he felt for her before becoming a widower, transformed itself into love. He commits the 'crime.' And immediately the 'accomplices' are frightened, they try to cross the French frontier. His 'son in uniform' denounces him, bears testimony against him during the trial. Result: fifteen months' hard labour.

"A sentence of the Tribunal of the Reich dated January 18th, 1938, condemns to ten months of hard labour young F. . . . , who is not a Jew, but who thought that he was one, when he committed the crime of letting himself be seduced by a fair German. This young man, who was legally the posthumous son of a Jew, married to a Christian, learnt during the trial that his mother, long before his birth, was the mistress of a pure Aryan, Dr. G. . . . 'Your father was for more than a year in the hospital, where he finally died,' the mother tearfully told him. 'I only saw him once a week in a common ward. My affair with Dr. G. . . . dates from that time.'

"The accused asks for his mother's and Dr. G.'s testimony. But according to jurisprudence, the intention suffices for the crime of 'Rassenschande' (race shame) to be committed. Not even the intention ! . . . The simple appearance, a preliminary to presumption ! . . .

"Take the case of Herr Samter, a Hindenburg (Upper Silesia) merchant, before the suppression of Jewish shops. He ought to be careful with that lady-client who, notwithstanding the bill 'Jude' in evidence in the shop window, did not hesitate to bargain over a radio set. This happened in the evening, just before the closing of the shop. And Samter was alone ! He should have found out about the lady's religion. She was a Fraulein Martha Waldbrun, who made him test several radio sets, not being able to make up her mind, leaning over the merchant's shoulder, under the excuse to make him explain a detail. . . . The policeman arrived. . . . During the trial Fraulein Waldbrun, seized with remorse, admitted that she had been paid by the police. Samter entirely absorbed by the sale of the set, did not make a single gesture, had not the slightest thought of gallantry. . . . Notwithstanding this fact, he is ruthlessly condemned to *six years'* hard labour. Horrified by the consequence of her act, Fraulein Waldbrun committed suicide. 'She did not want to survive her shame,' the newspapers declared.

" One could cite endless facts. . . . Not only must Jews not run the risk of giving life outside their race, they are also forbidden to save life. Before committing suicide, the famous specialist of children's diseases, Professor Knoepfelmacher of Vienna wrote the following words : 'I have saved the lives of 60,000 children ; to-day, I am obliged to take my own life.'

" Serotherapy, which saves thousands of children from diphtheria, was introducd in Germany by Von Behrend. Let German babies die rather than be healed by a Jew ! In two years the number of children victims of croup has risen from 3,992 in 1932 to 6,372 in 1934. . . . The parents of the tiny creature condemned to die, implore the Christian doctor to inject the salutary serum . . . the doctor trembles, for he remembers the terrible condemnation pronounced by Streicher : 'Serotherapy represents the specifically Jewish idea of soiling German blood with the blood of animals different from the human race.' "

The imagination can picture but a small part of what these manifold legal provisions, with their accompanying illegal excesses—ignoble parades of wretched men carrying mocking placards, Jewish cemeteries profaned by the hundreds, violence and humiliations of all sorts, confiscations of property, denunciations and travesties of justice—produce in the way of suffering and anguish, misery and dishonour for unfortunate human beings. Naturally, suicide thrives. The labour of teachers and propagandists poisons the hearts of the common people, of children, of the poor, with hate and contempt for Jews and other victims of persecution. But wait! Worst of all is the degradation of human dignity among the persecuted. Not only are there in some Berlin public squares yellow benches reserved for Jews; the worst is the fact that one may see Jews, sad weary Jews, sitting on these benches. And there have been families of a Jewish father and an Aryan mother in which children have extracted from the mother a confession of adultery in order to prove that they were born of pure Aryan blood and had a right to civic life.

But is there ever an end to lust and cruelty? These increase *ad infinitum*. New means of oppression are invented each day. Even the name of Jehovah has been proscribed. The racist persecution in the course of the year 1938 has produced spectacles which show that it is always possible to dishonour human nature *still further*.*

I know that Germany and racism are not necessarily identified and although such matters " go without saying," I must nevertheless note here that hate against a whole people would be a great madness, and that despite racism and the anti-Christianity which are ravaging German hearts, the humane reserves of Germanic culture are not exhausted. But if the moral cataclysms sweeping over a country must not prevent those who hope to secure thereby the peace of the world, from desiring political agreements

* See pp. 46 ff.

with that country, those same desires, in turn, must not prevent the truth from being uttered. The example of German antisemitism, which the National Socialist leaders conjured up and continue violently to provoke, and which they are simultaneously trying to regularise while welding it into a favoured instrument for influencing opinion in other countries, this example of antisemitism and its propaganda which is being furthered everywhere, in America as in Europe, are bad omens for such civilisation as remains to us. Italy, for political reasons, has begun to cultivate antisemitic sentiments, a novelty for her. Since the summer of 1938 Italian Fascism has become deliberately racist (I will return to this matter in a further section). Under moral and cultural forms, without overt brutality or legislative trappings, a very severe antisemitism existed in Austria before the *Anschluss*. Now the native country of the child Mozart is no more. The new events, which in recent months have changed the face of Central Europe, and to which I shall refer later, have been accompanied in these lands by a general and implacable surge of antisemitism.

Previously, other countries were already affected, Poland, of which I shall speak shortly, and also, to a lesser degree, Lithuania and Yugoslavia. Antisemitic propaganda, supported by Germany, is attempting to trouble many countries in South America.

In Rumania a wave of terror broke forth in the beginning of the year 1938.

The Jews in Rumania

The Jews of Rumania have long been treated as legal inferiors. Despite the promises made at the Congress of Berlin in 1878, it was only with the Treaty of 1919, following the world war and with the Constitution of the enlarged Rumanian State, that the equality of all Rumanian citizens before the law, "without distinction of race, language or religion," was proclaimed. In annexing Bessarabia, Bukovina, Transylvania, the Banat and Maramuresh, with some 9,000,000 inhabitants, Rumania undertook, in accord with a quite obvious rule of international public law, to recognise as entitled to the benefits of Rumanian law all the Jews, some 600,000, living in those territories.

I have but limited confidence in statistics, particularly the demographic statistics of countries subject to nationality conflicts and disputes. Relying, however, on the official data of the Rumanian statistical bureau, and rounding off figures upward rather than downward, it would seem reasonable to draw the following conclusions. Old Rumania counted some 250,000 Jews, long assimilated. Adding this figure to that which I just gave for the territories newly annexed, we see that before the war there were 850,000 Jews in the present domain of the kingdom of Rumania. To-day there are a few more or less, less rather than more,* that is, about 4½ per cent. of the total population. Of this number, it is estimated that some 10,000 are Jews who fled from Russia since the war and settled in Rumania "fraudulently." †

Nevertheless, in January and February, 1938, the officials in power announced the intention of withdrawing Rumanian

* According to the figures of the Bucharest Demographic Institute, the figure would be 760,000 to 765,000. Of these some 30,000 have, since 1920, been refused naturalisation ; these have only duties, and no rights, as Rumanian subjects. Their number is augmented by some thousands of others, whom the Liberal Cabinet of M. Tataresco, which preceded the antisemitic Government of M. Goga, deprived arbitrarily of their Rumanian citizenship.

† After the establishment of Nazism in Germany, a great number of German Jewish families *crossed* Rumania, which admitted them only in transit. Very few remained. The proportion of German Jews settled in the country since 1933 is insignificant.

nationality and the right of settlement and residence in the kingdom, from 500,000 Jews, accused by M. Goga of having entered the country by fraud, although King Carol would reckon the number at half this figure. The cry of reprobation was being raised not against 10,000 Jews, but against 500,000.

Thus, even for the best statistical sleight-of-hand artists, it was difficult to reconcile this project with the solemn obligation of the treaty of December 9th, 1919. Moreover, for what purpose ? The truth is that racism, for which the solemn pledges of treaties mean very little, was sweeping like a whirlwind through Rumania, and wanted to dispatch in the most rapid and brutal way not only 10,000 or 250,000 or 500,000 Jews, but the entire Jewish population of the country.

All Jewish citizens were barred from public posts. It was decided to close to Jews certain professions and businesses, to expropriate their agricultural enterprises, to exclude them from the theatre and cinemas, to take away from a large number of Jewish doctors, engineers, architects and lawyers, the right to practise their professions. It did not matter that the country districts suffered from a terrible shortage of doctors ; Jewish doctors must first be crushed. The three Jewish newspapers in Bucharest were suppressed. The lron Guard organised a reign of terror against Jewish students in the high schools and against Jewish attorneys. The Blueshirts inspired hatred against the Jews among the rural masses, hounded Jewish peasants by the hundreds, compelled them to flee wretchedly from their farms. And all this seemed a beginning only. The worst threats, a mortal terror, hung over hundreds of thousands of human beings for several weeks.

" Well," M. Octavian Goga told the two Tharaud

brothers, "couldn't we send them far away . . . some-where . . . to some island which they could never leave. . . . Warships of all countries could cruise around it. . . ." (The Goga Government was short-lived. It fell rapidly; and not long afterwards the newspapers announced the death of Monsieur Goga himself.)

It seems that in Rumania, Church and State collaborated in this new style of government, if one may rely on the declarations of the late Patriarch of the Orthodox Rumanian Church, Miron Cristea, published in a Bucharest news-paper.* There he expressed the opinion that Jews had "bled white" the Rumanian people, and would soon force the Rumanians to "abandon their homes and their hearths and wander through the world," and that there must be somewhere on the face of the globe, "in Africa, in Australia, in Asia, in the islands," some free land to which the Jews could be relegated. "I do not know enough about world geography to tell you where this country is," added this minister of the Gospel. He was to succeed M. Goga at the head of the Rumanian Govern-ment, and was obliged by political necessities to renounce that useful geographical inquiry, as well as the legal realisation of his wishes.

Let us recall the declaration adopted in 1931 by the Catholic Union of International Studies : " The members of a national group (that is, of a minority) are bound to observe all those duties and obligations toward the State of which they are subjects that Christian morality and politics impose on the conscience of citizens. They enjoy all the rights which both accord to the man and to the citizen." Monseigneur Beaupin recently wrote : "To reaffirm such principles, applicable to all lands and to all

* *Curentul*, August 19th, 1937.

times, is not to intervene in the internal politics of any particular State." Moreover, Rumania had the wisdom to reject the racist madness of the Goga Government. The Iron Guard, whose plots, inspired by Nazism, were threatening the Crown, was dissolved ; and severe judiciary sanctions were taken against its leader, who was later killed, according to the police report, while trying to escape from prison. The antisemitic mood remains very strong in this country, but the projects of legal persecution were abandoned.

The Jews in Poland

In Germany antisemitism has taken an anti-Christian form ; in Rumania it has taken an Orthodox form, strongly tinged with anti-Catholicism. At the Congress of the " Orthodox Brotherhood " held in November, 1937, speakers put Catholicism on a plane with Communism ; the Congress demanded the denunciation of the Papal Concordat, and denounced the Vatican's " aggressive and denationalising proselytism." Rumanian Catholics complain of being the object of calumnies and of campaigns o hatred which lead to religious war.

In Poland, on the other hand, although the heads of the Catholic Church, notably Cardinal Hlond, have repudiated " systematic and unconditional hostility toward the Jews," antisemitism has taken a Catholic form, from the fact that, sociologically, it is natural, all too natural, that passions, however misleading, which claim to defend a country's national interests, should claim also support from its traditional religion.

I am aware that in general Poland has rejected the doctrine of pagan racism and that its Government would like to limit the conflict to the economic field. I am aware that there are in Poland three to three and a half million Jews, a little more than 10 per cent. of the total population, so that the problems which I discussed at the beginning of this essay and which concerns countries with a large Jewish national minority, are more real for Poland than for any other country. Nevertheless, it remains a fact that intense antisemitism persists there, further stimulated by German influence and by the bad national economic situation. By heightening, on the one hand, ' touchy ' national suscepti-bilities, and, on the other, exasperated sufferings and claims, this antisemitism is likely to lead to quite insoluble diffi-culties. In recent years, particularly in 1937, the Polish Jews have suffered a persecution which, although not legally organised as in Germany, nevertheless tends to render life entirely impossible for them.

I hastily record—alas, it is always that same litany—the extensive boycott of Jewish merchants and artisans (what is called " dry " antisemitism),* the frightful multiplication of brawls, pillagings, pogroms with casualties of dead and wounded, systematic travesties of justice, a tragic increase in violence, blind popular hatreds. By letting loose against the Jews peasants dying of hunger, do they imagine that they will find a solution to the agrarian question and to rural pauperism ? A just redistribution of land, such as other States effected in order to head off worse develop-ments, is just what the great landowners wish to avoid at any price, and that is why they strive to turn the anger of

---

* Those who preach this mass boycott as an economic remedy for the atrophy of non-Jewish trade, forget that, however desirable it may be to replace the régime of free competition by one of organised communal labour, the operation of any given régime cannot be violently disturbed. In fact, the boycott in question is part of a scheme to reduce Jewish traders and artisans to famine, in order to force them to emigrate. (As though the Jews, especially those of Poland, were not predisposed to furnish a great quota of emigrants, *if only they could !* If only other countries would open their frontiers !) Such a boycott adds a spice of cruelty to a situation already deplorable enough for all. And what it certainly contrives to do is to develop evil passions without restraint.

the poor against the Jews. The most odious events are those which occur in circles that, presumably reserved to science and culture, transform themselves into the vehicles of racist influence, and provokers of passions. In January, 1937, there were university troubles on which I prefer, for the sake of the good name of the students of Warsaw, not to dwell at length. We know that recently, giving in to antisemitic pressure, the Polish university authorities have installed separate benches for Jewish students, thus creating ghettos in classrooms. Numerous Polish professors have protested against this measure, and some of them—like those Jewish students who, rather than sit on such benches, stand during lectures—have also insisted on lecturing on their feet.

I must add—I will not hide one aspect of the matter that pains me—that for sociological reasons to which I just alluded, it is generally the Catholic sections of the Polish population which seem most affected by antisemitism. Deplorable incitements have spread among them, and the Catholic Press has all too often been an accomplice. Often, too, there seems to be a spirit which, without endorsing excesses committed against Jews, resigns itself, and, without professing antisemitism, regards the Jewish drama with the indifference of the *reasonable* man who goes coldly along his way. But he is our fellow-creature, this wounded Jew lying half-dead on the road from Jerusalem to Jericho. . . .

And as for those believers who think they are serving Christianity by binding its cause to that of political, and violent, and unjust parties, we know that in reality they profoundly damage the cause they would serve.

To close this section, let me recall that, according to the Treaty of June 29th, 1919, the Polish Government is

obligated to " accord to all inhabitants full and entire
protection of life and liberty, without distinction as to
birth, nationality, race or religion." Article VII specifies
that " all Polish nationals shall be equal before the law and
shall enjoy identical civil and political rights, without
distinction of race, language or religion ; differences in
religion, creed or belief shall not be grounds for depriving
any Polish national of his enjoyment of any civil or political
rights, notably admission to public employment, offices or
honours, or the exercise of the various professions and
industries." This, we must grant, goes rather badly with
the *numerus clausus*, ghetto benches and the indulgence,
not to say worse, too often extended to pogromists by
judicial authorities.*

1938–1939

In the course of the year 1938 the situation of the Jews
throughout the world became still worse.

I will mention first the troubles and massacres in Palestine.
The short range policy, so long hesitant and weak, of the
mandate Power bears heavy responsibilities. More fundamentally, it may be that the ancient rivalry of Ishmael and
Israel demands, for its appeasement, a fraternal generosity
of which neither has shown himself capable since the
establishment of the Zionist home. Nor am I unaware
that this establishment was inevitably subject to the
capitalistic and colonist methods by which all such great
temporal realisations are impregnated in the world to-day.
On the other hand, the Jews, who have shown admirable
self-restraint (in spite of the theories of some extremists
who wanted to answer terrorism with terrorism), are

* On the question of the Jewish drama in Poland it will be useful to consult
the well-documented articles of Oscar de Ferenzy in *Juste Parole*, 1937 and 1938.

growing exasperated by three years of murders, lawlessness and complete governmental inefficiency; and a few terroristic acts may have been committed on their part, though these are the exception. The fact remains that the rights acquired by the heroic labour of the Jewish pioneers, as well as the rights granted to them after the war by international agreements, are unquestionable. The Jews in Palestine are suffering unjust violence, and there as elsewhere, sympathy must go first to the victims and not to the aggressors.

If persecution has subsided in Rumania—at least in respect of discriminatory laws and the violence that pro-German elements had been willing to provoke—Fascist Italy, on the other hand, has avowedly adopted racism in theory and practice. What reasons can be assigned to this surprising wave of official antisemitism in a country where the Jewish population is very small, has been established for centuries, and is remarkably assimilated? Must one not ascribe it to this weakness in its ideological and dynamic power that Fascism is compelled to be dragged along by the *élan* of its rival and ally, National-Socialist totalitarianism? Is it not reduced to imitating ostentatiously (while proclaiming that it owes nothing to anyone) the Hitlerian pseudo-mysticism of race and blood? Must one not think that antisemitism is for the Fascist chiefs merely a way of preparing a general policy which—naturally in the name of Latin and Christian civilisation—will place the sword of the Prophet in the hands of Il Duce? The fact is, in any event, that those who have, as we do, a reverence for Italian soil penetrated with humanity and civilisation, and who know all that the world and culture owe to the thinkers and artists of this admirable country and to the virtues of its people, feel a profound sorrow and shame in seeing its

D 2

present masters striving thus to debase its history. Already the most vexatious measures are being taken in Italy against the Jews; they are being thrown out of the positions they occupied in governmental and cultural spheres, and driven on a large scale out of economic activities. There too, as in Austria, one saw men, who had devoted their life to spiritual culture and to the progress of science and to whom the very right of existence was now denied, answer this barbarous negation by suicide. A legislative proposal, aimed at preventing the marriage of Jews and non-Jews, gave rise to a protest on the part of the Catholic Church, which declared it contrary to the concordat between it and the Italian State. If the Fascist legislators hesitate before this protest and tone down the juridical measures they had at first in mind, they will not give up, however, the intention of practically attaining their aim through diverted means. The great majority of the Italian population is disgusted with this imported antisemitism; but the leaders of the régime assert their firm determination to impose it by force and to aggravate it.

But it is in Germany that the spectacle is most tragic. Everyone recollects the events echoed in the Press of the world; what the public knows less well, however, is the depths of wickedness and contempt for the human person on the one side, and of sorrow and agony on the other. The annexation of Austria provoked an unprecedented wave of violence, and unbelievable scenes of sadistic cruelty. Measures of ruthless persecution condemn the Jews to slow death, and to despair. Persecutors were seen rejoicing at the suicides to which their ferocious actions led a great number of unfortunates—is this not a good method of racial selection? And who will tell of the ignominious treatment suffered in concentration camps by so many victims—Jews, Catholics, and political suspects ? The Catholic religion is, on the other hand, more and more seriously threatened, and the world can witness the inglorious collapse of the system of an Austrian State religion inherited from Josephism. Such Austrians as were blinded by the desire for power and who imagined that because they were more intelligent they could tame Nazism and politically profit by it, opposing at the same time its anti-religious excesses, are now dreadfully disappointed. Even the Austrian Nazis are disappointed. Besides, it may be that the Austrian temperament, with its sensitiveness and its fantasy and its suppleness (which, passive though it is, is really exhaustive of all methods of discipline), will provoke many an internal difficulty in the immense Prussian machinery which now holds it in its grip. Alas, Europeans still remember all that Austria represented for their civilisation ; they remember the mission which was Austria's, to improve the gifts of the Germanic mind in the direction of happiness and freedom, not of barbarism. The collapse of this country and its absorption by the German Reich, following the errors accumulated by the victors of the war of 1914–1918, and the retaliation that the vanquished demanded from the dark forces evoked by a political sorcery which surprised the universe, is one of the most sinister signs of the present epoch.

In her turn, Czechoslovakia, sacrificed in September, 1938, to Hitler's impatient lust in return for the peace of the world and for a delusive hope of European stabilisation (as if imperialist appetites and the principle of *international bad faith* could ever admit stabilisation), was completely dismembered in March, 1939, and annexed as a protectorate country of the German Empire. By this act, the Reich has crossed, so we may think, the threshold of the zone where history's Eumenides waits for the conquerors who are in too great a hurry. So far as the destiny of the Jews is concerned, the results of this annexation have been immediate. The German racial laws, with all their barbarism, are already in force for the German populations of the Czech country; and by contagion, the antisemitic mentality has gained the entire former Czechoslovakian territory.

Due to German influence, intense antisemitism also reigns in Hungary. The Catholic episcopate seeks to discourage enactment of the most violent legislative measures, but anti-Jewish passion and racist ideas have been unloosened. One may say that in persecuting the Jews, Hungary stands between Germany and Italy. Considering the situation occupied by Jews in commerce and industry, it appears that German antisemitic propaganda pursues in Hungaria, as in Central Europe in general, the most concrete and precise aims, which is to ruin or enslave the industrial activity of these regions, and in reducing their national economies to a strictly agricultural status, to transform them into granaries for German needs.

What Must Be Done?

We have just seen to what excesses antisemitism has gone in various countries, revealing itself as one of the sinister symptoms of the general deterioration of our civilisation, and ranging against the unfortunate and suffering, other men no less unfortunate and suffering.

In the face of such facts, is it possible to remain indifferent and inert? How can one escape the anxious question: *what must be done?* I realise that the world to-day resounds with the same question inspired by other horrors without number. But that is no reason for us to shut ourselves off.

Everything must be done, every possible remedy tried, however insufficient each may seem by itself.

The President of the Polish Council, General Skladkowski, recently said: " In the name of the Polish Government I declare that we will oppose with all our might every pogrom and campaign of hatred such as arose last year against the Jews. There is no place among us for racial struggles. There is merely a problem of over-population, lying within the economic field alone." At the same time, the Budget Director of the Ministry of the Interior called on the colonial Powers for " material and financial aid to Poland for the solution of the problem of Jewish emigration, with the co-operation of the Jews themselves." *

Emigration is therefore one of the proposed cures. To tell the truth, it would not, at its best, be more than a partial remedy. It would bring some mitigation to the economic crisis of Eastern Europe by compensating, at least, for population increase resulting from births, perhaps even by cutting slightly the absolute total of the local Jewish population. The idea of mass emigration of all the Jews of Central and Eastern Europe is however absolutely out of the question because it is impossible.

But the tragedy is that, even reduced to these proportions and considered with reference only to a relatively small part of the Jewish population, emigration to-day faces major obstacles. All countries are closing their frontiers to emigrants. Here we are facing the general phenomenon so fatal to civilisation, that of the turning in of nations upon themselves. As far as the Jews are concerned, Dr. Ruppin, Professor at the Hebrew University of Jerusalem, has observed some years ago that " the period of mass migra-

* *La Croix*, January 25th, 1938.

tions, which transformed Jewish life during the last fifty years, must be regarded as closed. Emigration can at most take 30,000 to 40,000 Jews annually out of Eastern Europe, that is to say, only one-third of their normal annual population increase (in all the countries of Eastern Europe). One must ask whether, in such conditions, the economic position of the Jews in Eastern Europe, especially in Poland, is not threatened with veritable catastrophe since, during the last fifty years, emigration alone made it bearable." The same conclusion, then, is reached on the Jewish as on the Polish side.

Thus it would seem that, in the interests of all, the civilised community must take hold of itself. A special effort must be made, despite all obstacles, to facilitate some resumption, as large as possible, of Jewish emigration, that is, of voluntary emigration. And how? On the one hand, we look to Zionism, toward which, moreover, the Polish Government has long shown itself favourable. But we realise the present difficulties in the Palestinian home, which can unfortunately take in only a small quota of immigrants. On the other hand, nations, especially certain large nations possessing sparsely inhabited territories, must resume a broader policy of immigration, thanks to an appropriate international organisation *; the scanty generosity which certain countries, as, for example, Australia, have shown in this matter, is detrimental not only to Jews, but also to humanity at large.

* For a general consideration of these problems, independent of the Jewish question, see *L'Homme Réel*, February–March, 1936, and several articles by Magdeleine Paz and Madame Ancelet-Hustache. In France, a bill for a law concerning immigrants was filed on December 11th, 1934. Several law-decrees (*décrets-lois*) concerning foreigners have been passed in 1938, but they do not go beyond the framework of police measures, antecedent to a true policy of immigration. It must be observed that the figure of foreign population, due to political emigration from many European countries, amounts in France to about three million. This fact gives rise to serious problems.

Finally, if necessary, settlement in certain colonial territories must be resorted to. That method presents special difficulties, due on one hand to the climatic conditions, often extremely bad, of some of the colonial lands intended for immigrants, and on the other hand, to the indispensible financial and economic equipment. I do not think, however, that these difficulties must be considered insurmountable. So far as France is concerned, the opening of Madagascar or of some other colonial territories, as, for instance, Guiana, to a fixed quota of Jewish emigrants has at times been suggested. I believe that if solid and well elaborated offers were made in this direction to the French Government (and no doubt these offers might be so conceived as incidentally to serve national interests), this Government would be disposed to examine them favourably. The same hope may be held in regard to the other colonial Powers.*

German antisemitic policy has recently made the question of emigration still more urgent, although in reality, Jewish emigration has for Germany much less demographic interest than for Poland. But the aim here was to improve her economic situation in bartering Jews for money or merchandise. Whatever these mercantile motives may be, it is the conflagration of hatred enflamed by German racism that renders the situation so full of anguish. If some world catastrophe does not alter radically and tragically the terms of all the problems of to-day, this question of Jewish emigration must be regarded as one which unconditionally equires a prompt solution for the entire Western world.

* If the demographic problem of Europe were considered in all its ramifications, one might be led to the idea of a general arrangement for the utilisation and settlement of the vast colonisation territories for the general benefit of the European and native populations. But such an idea would presuppose a true European community, and there again economics would appear to depend on morality and on politics.

Here we must consider not simply the Jewish demographic problem in itself, but also the terrible threat which antisemitic passions, blindly encouraged by some governments, add to it. If it were possible now to bring forth and decide upon the absorption of a portion of the Jewish population over several decades, not only would a real if partial relief result for the Jewish and non-Jewish populations of Eastern Europe, but perhaps there might transpire a sort of political and psychological purgation of antisemitic passions in the countries which are to-day in paroxysms.

I want to add that the insanity of antisemitism here displays itself strikingly : on the one hand, it persecutes the Jews in order to force them to emigrate, although the Jews have always provided a high percentage of emigrants and are prevented to-day only by a material obstacle, the general closing of frontiers. On the other hand, confirming a statement made at the outset of this essay, it adds one more obstacle to that emigration at which it aims, as well as to any real settlement of the Jewish problem. Because emigration, like any other settlement, presupposes the co-operation of the Jews themselves, and hence an atmosphere of understanding and collaboration. In addition, it does not seem possible that the difficulties presented by emigration, particularly to colonial countries, can be solved under prevailing economic conditions unless Jewish international welfare organisations were disposed to finance in part the settlement of emigrants who are without resources.

And yet, as far as antisemitic persecutions are concerned, the remedy we have been discussing, emigration, can at best be a mere palliative. Is there anything else to be considered ? The fact remains that the great mass of the Jewish population must, in the best of cases, necessarily abide where it is. Millions of human beings cannot be expelled to become wanderers, men without a country. Are they to be driven to die of hunger? Are they all to be massacred? The more public opinion everywhere is informed and awakened, the more one can hope that persecution will lose ground. Legally, the Jewish populations may appeal to constitutional and international guarantees which have been extended to them. And it is up to the governments of countries for whom the word justice still has some meaning, to act, supported by public opinion, to compel respect for treaties which bear their signatures. The League of Nations, which showed itself so weak in so many cases, took up the case of the Jews of Rumania during the Goga Ministry. The United States has done much and can do much more for the protection of the Jewish populations. The wave of indignation raised in the United States by the Nazi persecution in the autumn of 1938 was formidable and accompanied by energetic action and efficacious measures of assistance, which merit the gratitude of all men of feeling.

And what then? Then one may hope that the entire civilised world, if it succeeds in escaping a general catastrophe, or perhaps having experienced one, will come to know a fundamentally new and a more just order. For it seems that matters have reached a pass where nothing can be remedied unless everything is transformed. This conclusion, of course, is one which brings little relief to those who are in torment to-day.

There remains for all us, Jews and Christians, to turn toward the invisible powers residing in the heart of man, toward the springs of history which lie within ourselves, in order to purify those springs.

If we but realised to what point external events and the

forms of things depend on the invisible images which our free wills delineate within us, we would have more confidence in spiritual means.

At the same time, we would give up fighting hatred with hatred. We would understand what has been so often affirmed by Gandhi, the real power, even over political and social realities, of love and truth.

Perhaps I may be allowed to address a special appeal to our friends in Poland. They know that I have been careful to say nothing here which might wound them. If Poland manages to overcome, by a splendid rallying of its finest forces, the apparently irremediable conflicts to which the Jewish problem gives rise there, a great example will have been given to Europe.

According to the words of the President of the Polish Council which I just cited, there is no room among the Poles for racial conflicts. Let them realise that the union of all elements of the population is more essential for national prosperity in that country than it is anywhere else. Let them recall the declaration of Marshal Pilsudski on the reopening of the University of Warsaw, when he affirmed that, after having suffered oppression and persecution for more than a century, Poles could not harbour hates between groups of different nationality and origin. There is a real problem in Poland, and it is above all economic and social, and its real solution is to be found in the advance of social justice and of economic equipment. On this road, the co-operation of the Jewish element is not to be under-rated.

If they will dedicate the same energy to construction and invention as now goes into controversy, there would be a way for Jews and non-Jews to live on the same earth, perhaps in equal poverty, and to aid each other by brotherly labour. It has been said that " Jews and Poles must

54

contrive to live together willy-nilly, since they are compelled to do so by fate." They will do so more profitably for the country if they arrange things *voluntarily*. Even with respect to economic categories, the problem here, too, is primarily of a moral order.

Polish Catholics, by entering deeply into the spirit of the reasons which have led their bishops, following the example of the Pope, to condemn Chauvinism, pagan Racism and antisemitism, along with Communism, should, it is hoped, understand that it is not enough to abstain in a heaven of spiritual exaltation from hating Jews as such, while conceding to their enemies all the legends, the prejudices, the heated arguments in whose name they are persecuted on an earth of temporal realities. No ! they must, in response to the general Christian and human vocation, descend with the grace of God and His justice to the very depths of mundane woes and conflicts, the very depths of this one as of all others ! Then will they give justice its chance, and many other things will be added unto them.

As to ourselves, wherever we are, we all bear responsibility inasmuch as the drama of human history is like a visible projection of that which is happening within ourselves. There is nothing more urgent than that secret labour by which those with *a little faith* raise, first of all in themselves, the level of mankind's spiritual energy. Such labour is effective, it brings forth tangible fruits more quickly than is realised.

There are in contemporary Europe those who, in order to fan the evil flame now consuming nations, are decreeing extermination and death, and first of all that of the Jews— because it is this they want, after all, is it not ? Under the stupid apparatus of scientific Racism or forged documents, they conceal from others and sometimes from themselves, their mad dream of a general massacre of the race of Moses and Jesus. This massacre remains a dream ; but the germs of hate with which it pollutes the atmosphere are a reality. A very large measure of love, justice and charity is required to cleanse that atmosphere.

Our times offer unparalleled banquets to the demons of cruelty. Stalin gave them the Kulaks, Hitler gives them the Jews. Each one of us will have his turn perhaps. The immense clamour which arises from the German concentration camps, as well as from the Russian, is not perceptible to our ears, but it penetrates the secret fibres of the life of the world, and its invisible vibration tears them apart.

Never before in the history of the world were the Jews persecuted so universally ; and never has persecution attacked, as to-day, both Jews and Christians. We can see here a sign that we have entered upon an apocalyptic period of history ; this is also a sign that we must shape our means to the conditions of such a period. For a long time an all too human civilisation puts its trust in material forces, while invoking—not always hypocritically—equity and the spirit. To-day these material forces have been brought to the state of barbarism, and this is only the natural result of that perverted mentality which, in its delusory belief that through them it could reign supreme, put everything in their power. In order to face the violence thus let loose, men of freedom must not renounce the means which lay at their disposal in material energies, provided that these are subordinated to the spirit of justice ; but they can no longer put their confidence in them, since the world itself summons them finally to put their trust in love and truth alone.

Nowadays, for political ends, there is a remarkable abuse of names still dear to us, names in which even the most crushed of men still places hope. In some countries people "buy Christian" in order to boycott the Jewish merchant. Hating the Gospel, the dominant currents of German National Socialism proclaim themselves Christians—against the Pope and the churches. In Rumania M. Goga's party, if I am not mistaken, called itself National Christian, while that of M. Cuza was the League for Christian Defence. Perhaps some day there will be a Christian racism, perhaps Thors and Odins of Christian civilisation, Christian mustard gas, and Christian bombardments of open cities. Men vie with each other to hound from this unhappy planet God's sanctity, blasphemed by some, profaned by others. The despair into which many souls are in danger of being plunged by these things is heavy with malediction. It is not thus that Christian civilisation can be defended. I do not believe that I am indulging in national self-satisfaction when I say that the Catholics of France heard with particular fervour what Pope Pius XI told their Bishops at Christmas, 1937: "The preaching of the truth did not win many victories for Christ; it led to the Cross. It was by charity that he saved souls and led them to follow him." These words apply to Christians of the entire world. There is no other way for us to gain our own soul, and the souls of others, as well as a little peace for the world.

FINIS